THIRTY
DISCIPLESHIP EXERCISES

The Pathway to Christian Maturity

A Bible Study for

Small Groups

and Personal Ministry

This study was originally prepared by Charlie Riggs, Director of Counseling and Follow-Up for the Billy Graham Evangelistic Association from 1957 to 1989.

Thirty Discipleship Exercises
Copyright © 1980, 1982, 1987, 1992, 1994 (revised 1998, 2002)
Billy Graham Evangelistic Association
Two Parkway Plaza
4828 Parkway Plaza Blvd. , Suite 200
Charlotte, N.C. 28217

Table of Contents

Forward

WHO IS JESUS CHRIST?

You may be picking up this book for several reasons. Are you a Christian who wants to grow in your faith? Or maybe you have just recently committed your life to Jesus Christ? Or you may simply be curious about what it means to have a relationship with Jesus Christ and want to know more. Jesus came to earth as God in human form. He came to enable us to have a relationship with Him—to bridge the gap between humanity and God.

This study will help you understand what it means to commit your life to Christ, have a real relationship with Him, and be sure of spending eternity in heaven with Him.

The first lesson in your study will deal with salvation, which simply means deliverance from sin and its consequences. The Holy Spirit works in your life when you have a relationship with Christ. In the lesson you will find six verses from the Bible that teach us about salvation.

The first verse is found in Philippians 2:5–7: "*Christ Jesus, who, being in very nature God, did not consider equality with God something to be grasped, but made himself nothing, taking the very nature of a servant, being made in human likeness.*" Jesus Christ, who has always existed as God, determined to come to earth so He could rescue us from our sins by dying on a cross. The birth of Christ was necessary so that He could be both God and human. Christmas is celebrated around the world as the birth of Christ. On Christmas we celebrate the direct intervention of God into human history. The other five verses deal with the process of the new birth of a believer in Christ.

Christ died for our sins according to the Scriptures, He was buried and He was raised on the third day (1 Corinthians 15:3–4). Good Friday, signifying the death of Jesus, and Easter Sunday, the resurrection of Jesus, are likewise celebrated around the world.

Another step in the process of the new birth of a Christian is found in 2 Corinthians 5:21: "*God made him [Christ Jesus] who had no sin to be sin for us, so that in him [or through Christ Jesus] we might become the righteousness of*

God." Right in God's sight—ready for Heaven.

Another link is found in 1 Timothy 2:5–6: *"For there is one God and one mediator between God and men, the man Christ Jesus, who gave himself as a ransom for all men."* Picture a great chasm with you on one side and God on the other. The Cross on which Jesus died bridges the gap. You cross that bridge through faith in Jesus.

Finally, *"Jesus did many other miraculous signs in the presence of his disciples, which are not recorded in this book. But these are written that you may believe that Jesus is the Christ, the Son of God, and that by believing you may have life in his name"* (John 20:30–31).

Go ahead—enjoy your lessons as you discover more about the Lord and Savior, Jesus Christ, and your daily walk with Him.

Introduction

Thirty Discipleship Exercises is a study featuring 30 different topics with six Bible verses for each lesson. The Scriptures selected are basic to the Christian life and witness. This material can be used for personal devotions, one-on-one discipling of another, or for small group discussions.

Personal Devotions

Take one topic a day for a 30-day period. Take at least 15 minutes each day to . . .

- Prayerfully read each verse.
- Circle key words or phrases. This will make you look more closely at the content of each verse.
- Answer the questions at the bottom of each page. You may want to use a separate sheet of paper or a small notebook for your written work.
- The verse study will give you a good look at some basic truth and specific insight to apply to everyday life.
- Memorize the verse in each lesson that is marked with an asterisk.

Once you have finished the exercises you can start all over again. The second time, open your Bible and look at each verse in its context—reading the whole chapter from which the verse is taken.

One-On-One Discipleship

You can use this material for meeting with an individual for personalized follow-up. Have the individual complete the exercises on a weekly basis.

When you meet, compare key words and phrases as well as answers to the questions. Discuss the application of these principles and have prayer together.

Small Group Study

The primary intention of these lessons is for small group interaction. A small group or **"Discovery Group"** is a group of 6–12 people meeting weekly in an informal setting to study and discuss the Word of God. The leader asks questions to draw the group into a discussion of the Bible study which each member of the group prepares in advance.

Each participant will be discovering biblical truth by:
- Circling key words or phrases
- Answering questions
- Defining key words
- Paraphrasing a verse
- Making application to daily life

What is the purpose of a Discovery Group?

The primary purpose is to follow up inquirers from an evangelistic event or a special outreach ministry. Following the evangelistic ministry people who have made commitments, their friends and other church members who are interested in Bible study should be invited to attend the Discovery Group.

Leadership and materials

Churches wishing to be in a Discovery Group ministry are responsible for training leaders. Copies of *Thirty Discipleship Exercises*, a part of the Christian Growth Series, can be purchased at your local bookstore or through Grason/World Wide Publications in Minneapolis, Minnesota, by calling (612) 333-0725, (800) 487-0433, e-mail: grasoncs@bgea.org, web page: www.grason.org.

Tips for Leaders are in the back of the book, pages 73–76. This section will be helpful in leading and organizing a study.

Format for a Discovery Group

There is no perfect size for a small group nor a perfect number of weeks for the group to meet. But experience has taught a helpful guideline—avoid too many and too much! Six to twelve persons skillfully led for seven weeks can provide a wonderful learning experience—a journey of discovery!

The first seven topics covered in this book are foundational to the Christian life . . . SALVATION—ASSURANCE—LORDSHIP—THE BIBLE—PRAYER—THE HOLY SPIRIT'S INDWELLING—WITNESS. In each lesson the Bible is the text and the Holy Spirit the teacher. All members of the group, including the leader, learn together. Indeed, every program of study must have a goal or objective. In each lesson in *Thirty Discipleship Exercises* we have three:

GOAL #1   DISCOVERY
"What does God say?"

GOAL #2   UNDERSTANDING
"What does the Scripture mean?"

GOAL #3   APPLICATION
"How can this affect my life?"

Following is a suggested plan for Lesson One—Salvation—and a basic guide for Lessons Two to Seven.

5

Lesson One—Salvation

A Suggested Plan for Week One

INTRODUCTION

An Opening Prayer

- The leader welcomes each member of the group and leads in an opening prayer.
- The leader then explains that the Bible study will cover seven lessons—New Beginnings—with each lesson requiring about 75 minutes.

3–5 Minutes

Get Acquainted

- **Starting with the leader,** have each group member give his or her name and special interest. EXAMPLE: Hobby, vacation, club activity, if a student, where? What program of study? etc.
- As each person shares, have each member write out the name and special interest on "My Group," page 9.
- Explain the importance of the six items under "As a member of the Discovery Group I will."

10–15 Minutes

THE LESSON—DISCUSSION

- The leader reads aloud the introductory paragraph on SALVATION, page 12.
- The leader then reads aloud slowly and carefully the six verses printed on the page. As you read, have group members circle words and phrases that seem to "jump off the page," either as an insight into spiritual truth or as a question.
- Take two or three minutes for the group to silently reread the six verses.
- Ask question number 2 in the shaded area. Discussion should follow after each question.

25–30 Minutes

THE LESSON—VERSE STUDY

Do the verse study on page 13. This will allow each group member to "dig deeper" into the subject of SALVATION.

- Have each member define "believe" and "eternal life."
- Ask if two or three members would like to share their definitions and have a brief discussion.
- Next, have each member paraphrase—that is write in their own words—the verse John 3:16. Have two or three members read aloud their paraphrases and have discussion.
- Next, have each member answer the question: *How can you apply the truth of this verse to your life today?* **Note:** This is usually more difficult in the beginning; therefore, the leader should set the pace by answering this question honestly and sensitively.

HOME ASSIGNMENT

Give the following home assignment in preparation for Lesson 2, ASSURANCE.

- Have each group member read the introduction paragraph and verses prior to next week.
- Have each group member write out a question(s) they would like to ask the group next week.
- Encourage each member to memorize John 3:16—salvation. Memory verse cards are in the back of the book.

FINALLY

- Thank everyone for their participation and lead in a closing prayer.
- Be careful *not* to put anyone on the spot by asking them to pray. Learning to pray out loud takes time. The leader should set a good example.

Total Time = 75 Minutes

A Suggested Plan for Leading Lessons 2–7

- Opening Prayer
  and get acquainted

  5–10 Minutes

- Review Memory Verse
  from previous week(s)

  3–5 Minutes

- The Lesson—Discussion
  and Verse Study

  40–50 Minutes

- Next week's home assignment

  3–5 Minutes

- Closing prayer time

  5 Minutes

Total Time = 75 Minutes

My Group

Members' Names	Special Interest/Prayer Needs
_____	_____
_____	_____
_____	_____
_____	_____
_____	_____
_____	_____
_____	_____
_____	_____
_____	_____
_____	_____
_____	_____

As a member of the Discovery Group I will:

1. Give priority to attending each week unless unavoidably hindered.
2. Faithfully complete the weekly home study assignments.
3. Participate in the group discussion as I am able.
4. Find creative ways to communicate my faith in Christ to others.
5. Pray by name for each member of my group during the weeks the group is meeting.
6. Refrain from discussing needs expressed in the group with anyone outside the group.

Signed: _____

Date: _____

New Beginnings

*A seven-week small group study
in the basics
of the Christian life.*

one
Salvation

Salvation means deliverance from sin and its consequence. Review and meditate on these truths until you can say with confidence, "I know I am a Christian . . . I have been born into God's family as His child . . . I now have eternal life."

1. Circle key words and phrases in the following Scriptures.

Christ Jesus, Who, being in very nature God, did not consider equality with God something to be grasped, but made himself nothing, taking the very nature of a servant, being made in human likeness. And being found in appearance as a man, he humbled himself and became obedient to death—even death on a cross! PHILIPPIANS 2:5–8

But God demonstrates his own love for us in this: While we were still sinners, Christ died for us. ROMANS 5:8

For what I received I passed on to you as of first importance: that Christ died for our sins according to the Scriptures, and that he was buried, that he was raised on the third day according to the Scriptures. 1 CORINTHIANS 15:3–4

For it is by grace you have been saved, through faith—and this not from yourselves, it is the gift of God—not by works, so that no one can boast. EPHESIANS 2:8–9

Yet to all who received him, to those who believed in his name, he gave the right to become children of God—children born not of natural descent, nor of human decision or a husband's will, but born of God. JOHN 1:12–13

* *For God so loved the world that he gave his one and only Son, that whoever believes in him shall not perish but have eternal life.* JOHN 3:16

2. In the above Scriptures, what do we learn about (answer briefly):

Jesus Christ *(Philippians 2:6–8)*
Salvation *(Romans 5:8; Ephesians 2:8–9; I Corinthians 15:3–4)*
Becoming God's Child *(John 1:12–13)*
Eternal Life *(John 3:16)*

3. Do a verse study using the form on the next page.

4. Memorize John 3:16.

Verse Study Form

Using the suggested memory verse marked with an asterisk from the opposite page, complete this verse study form.

1. Verse reference _____

2. List two key words and define them.
Key Word _____
Definition _____
_____

Key Word _____
Definition _____
_____

3. What does the verse say?
(Paraphrase—Rewrite the verse in your own words.)

_____
_____
_____
_____
_____
_____

4. How can you apply the truth of this verse to your life today?

_____
_____
_____
_____
_____
_____

Closing (Prayer time and assignment for next week)

two

Assurance

One of Satan's tricks is to cause believers to doubt their salvation. Having assurance means being certain with a freedom from doubt. Meditate on the following Scriptures to enable you to have victory over your doubts.

1. Circle key words and phrases in the following Scriptures.

In him we have redemption through his blood, the forgiveness of sins, in accordance with the riches of God's grace.   EPHESIANS 1:7

Who through faith are shielded by God's power until the coming of the salvation that is ready to be revealed in the last time.   1 PETER 1:5

For I am convinced that neither death nor life, neither angels nor demons, neither the present nor the future, nor any powers, neither height nor depth, nor anything else in all creation, will be able to separate us from the love of God that is in Christ Jesus our Lord.   ROMANS 8:38–39

My sheep listen to my voice; I know them, and they follow me. I give them eternal life, and they shall never perish; no one can snatch them out of my hand. My Father, who has given them to me, is greater than all; no one can snatch them out of my Father's hand.   JOHN 10:27–29

I write these things to you who believe in the name of the Son of God so that you may know that you have eternal life.   1 JOHN 5:13

* *Being confident of this, that he who began a good work in you will carry it on to completion until the day of Christ Jesus.*   PHILIPPIANS 1:6

2. What do we learn about assurance in (answer briefly):

> *Ephesians 1:7*   *John 10:27–29*
> *1 Peter 1:5*   *1 John 5:13*
> *Romans 8:38–39*   *Philippians 1:6*

3. Do a verse study using the form on the next page.

4. Memorize Philippians 1:6.

14

Verse Study Form

Using the suggested memory verse marked with an asterisk from the opposite page, complete this verse study form.

1. Verse reference _____

2. List two key words and define them.
Key Word _____
Definition _____
_____

Key Word _____
Definition _____
_____

3. What does the verse say?
(Paraphrase—Rewrite the verse in your own words.)

_____
_____
_____
_____
_____
_____

4. How can you apply the truth of this verse to your life today?

_____
_____
_____
_____
_____
_____

Closing (Prayer time and assignment for next week)

three
Lordship

When we place our faith in Jesus Christ, He becomes not only our Savior but also our Sovereign Lord and Master. We are under new ownership. We can only enjoy our new life in Christ as we daily seek His will and follow Him in obedience.

1. Circle key words and phrases in the following Scriptures.

Do you not know that your body is a temple of the Holy Spirit, who is in you, whom you have received from God? You are not your own; you were bought at a price. Therefore honor God with your body.

1 CORINTHIANS 6:19–20

Jesus replied: "'Love the Lord your God with all your heart and with all your soul and with all your mind.' This is the first and greatest commandment."

MATTHEW 22:37–38

* *Delight yourself in the LORD and he will give you the desires of your heart. Commit your way to the LORD; trust in him and he will do this.*

PSALM 37:4–5

But seek first his kingdom and his righteousness, and all these things will be given to you as well. MATTHEW 6:33

I am the vine; you are the branches. If a man remains in me and I in him, he will bear much fruit; apart from me you can do nothing. JOHN 15:5

Why do you call me, "Lord, Lord," and do not do what I say? LUKE 6:46

2. From the above passages, what do we learn about (answer briefly):

New Ownership   Priorities
Obedience   Benefits

3. Do a verse study using the form on the next page.

4. Memorize Psalm 37:4–5.

Verse Study Form

Using the suggested memory verse marked with an asterisk from the opposite page, complete this verse study form.

1. Verse reference _____

2. List two key words and define them.

Key Word _____

Definition _____

_____

Key Word _____

Definition _____

_____

3. What does the verse say?
(Paraphrase—Rewrite the verse in your own words.)

_____

_____

_____

_____

_____

_____

4. How can you apply the truth of this verse to your life today?

_____

_____

_____

_____

_____

_____

Closing (Prayer time and assignment for next week)

The Bible

four

To be the kind of Christians God wants us to be, we need to know and obey the Scriptures. Make it your habit to memorize and meditate on the Word of God daily.

1. Circle key words and phrases in the following Scriptures.

But his delight is in the law of the LORD, and on his law he meditates day and night. He is like a tree planted by streams of water, which yields its fruit in season and whose leaf does not wither. Whatever he does prospers.
PSALM 1:2–3

Your word is a lamp to my feet and a light for my path. PSALM 119:105

The unfolding of your words gives light; it gives understanding to the simple. PSALM 119:130

Great peace have they who love your law, and nothing can make them stumble. PSALM 119:165

And how from infancy you have known the holy Scriptures, which are able to make you wise for salvation through faith in Christ Jesus. All Scripture is God-breathed and is useful for teaching, rebuking, correcting and training in righteousness. 2 TIMOTHY 3:15–16

* *Do not merely listen to the word, and so deceive yourselves. Do what it says.* JAMES 1:22

2. What do we learn about the value of Scripture in (answer briefly):

Psalm 1:2–3   Psalm 119:165
Psalm 119:105   2 Timothy 3:15–16
Psalm 119:130   James 1:22

3. Do a verse study using the form on the next page.

4. Memorize James 1:22.

Verse Study Form

Using the suggested memory verse marked with an asterisk from the opposite page, complete this verse study form.

1. Verse reference _____

2. List two key words and define them.

Key Word _____

Definition _____

_____

Key Word _____

Definition _____

_____

3. What does the verse say?

(Paraphrase—Rewrite the verse in your own words.)

_____

_____

_____

_____

_____

_____

4. How can you apply the truth of this verse to your life today?

_____

_____

_____

_____

_____

_____

Closing (Prayer time and assignment for next week)

five Prayer

Prayer is our lifeline to God. We need to form the habit of starting each day with prayer and then praying throughout the day.

1. Circle key words and phrases in the following Scriptures.

* *Until now you have not asked for anything in my name. Ask and you will receive, and your joy will be complete.* JOHN 16:24

Ask and it will be given to you; seek and you will find; knock and the door will be opened to you. MATTHEW 7:7

Call to me and I will answer you and tell you great and unsearchable things you do not know. JEREMIAH 33:3

Now to him who is able to do immeasurably more than all we ask or imagine, according to his power that is at work within us. EPHESIANS 3:20

Dear friends, if our hearts do not condemn us, we have confidence before God and receive from him anything we ask, because we obey his commands and do what pleases him. 1 JOHN 3:21–22

This is the confidence we have in approaching God: that if we ask anything according to his will, he hears us. And if we know that he hears us—whatever we ask—we know that we have what we asked of him. 1 JOHN 5:14–15

2. What do we learn about prayer in (answer briefly):

John 16:24   Ephesians 3:20
Matthew 7:7   1 John 3:21–22
Jeremiah 33:3   1 John 5:14–15

3. Do a verse study using the form on the next page.

4. Memorize John 16:24.

Verse Study Form

Using the suggested memory verse marked with an asterisk from the opposite page, complete this verse study form.

1. Verse reference _____

2. List two key words and define them.
Key Word _____
Definition _____
_____

Key Word _____
Definition _____
_____

3. What does the verse say?
(Paraphrase—Rewrite the verse in your own words.)

_____
_____
_____
_____
_____
_____

4. How can you apply the truth of this verse to your life today?

_____
_____
_____
_____
_____

Closing (Prayer time and assignment for next week)

six

The Holy Spirit's Indwelling

God has not left us alone in the world. His Holy Spirit lives in us and daily ministers to our needs.

1. Circle key words and phrases in the following Scriptures.

The wind blows wherever it pleases. You hear its sound, but you cannot tell where it comes from or where it is going. So it is with everyone born of the Spirit.   JOHN 3:8

Don't you know that you yourselves are God's temple and that God's Spirit lives in you?   1 CORINTHIANS 3:16

The Spirit himself testifies with our spirit that we are God's children. Now if we are children, then we are heirs—heirs of God and co-heirs with Christ, if indeed we share in his sufferings in order that we may also share in his glory.   ROMANS 8:16–17

Because those who are led by the Spirit of God are sons of God.
                                                          ROMANS 8:14

* *But the Counselor, the Holy Spirit, whom the Father will send in my name, will teach you all things and will remind you of everything I have said to you.*   JOHN 14:26

In the same way, the Spirit helps us in our weakness. We do not know what we ought to pray for, but the Spirit himself intercedes for us with groans that words cannot express.   ROMANS 8:26

2. What do we learn about the Holy Spirit in (answer briefly):

John 3:8	*Romans 8:14*
1 Corinthians 3:16	*John 14:26*
Romans 8:16–17	*Romans 8:26*

3. Do a verse study using the form on the next page.

4. Memorize John 14:26.

Verse Study Form

Using the suggested memory verse marked with an asterisk from the opposite page, complete this verse study form.

1. Verse reference _____

2. List two key words and define them.
Key Word _____
Definition _____

_____

Key Word _____
Definition _____

_____

3. What does the verse say?
(Paraphrase—Rewrite the verse in your own words.)

_____

_____

_____

_____

_____

_____

4. How can you apply the truth of this verse to your life today?

_____

_____

_____

_____

_____

_____

Closing (Prayer time and assignment for next week)

seven
Witness

When we become children of God through faith in Jesus Christ, we become responsible to tell others about Christ. There is no greater privilege than sharing the love of God with your friends, family and neighbors.

1. Circle key words and phrases in the following Scriptures.

"Come, follow me," Jesus said, "and I will make you fishers of men."
MATTHEW 4:19

In the same way, let your light shine before men, that they may see your good deeds and praise your Father in heaven. MATTHEW 5:16

* *But in your hearts set apart Christ as Lord. Always be prepared to give an answer to everyone who asks you to give the reason for the hope that you have. But do this with gentleness and respect.* 1 PETER 3:15

For we cannot help speaking about what we have seen and heard. . . . Believe in the Lord Jesus, and you will be saved—you and your household.
ACTS 4:20; 16:31

But you will receive power when the Holy Spirit comes on you; and you will be my witnesses in Jerusalem, and in all Judea and Samaria, and to the ends of the earth. ACTS 1:8

We are therefore Christ's ambassadors, as though God were making his appeal through us. We implore you on Christ's behalf: Be reconciled to God. 2 CORINTHIANS 5:20

2. What do we learn about our responsibility as witnesses in (answer briefly):

Matthew 4:19	*Acts 4:20 and 16:31*
Matthew 5:16	*Acts 1:8*
1 Peter 3:15	*2 Corinthians 5:20*

3. Do a verse study using the form on the next page.

4. Memorize 1 Peter 3:15.

Verse Study Form

Using the suggested memory verse marked with an asterisk from the opposite page, complete this verse study form.

1. Verse reference _____

2. List two key words and define them.
   Key Word _____
   Definition _____

   _____

   Key Word _____
   Definition _____

   _____

3. What does the verse say?
   (Paraphrase—Rewrite the verse in your own words.)

   _____

   _____

   _____

   _____

   _____

   _____

4. How can you apply the truth of this verse to your life today?

   _____

   _____

   _____

   _____

   _____

   _____

   Closing (Prayer time and assignment for next week)

Continuing
the Walk

eight
Jesus Christ: His Person and Work

Jesus Christ is the most unique person in all of history. He is the eternal God who became man in order that He could die for the sins of the world. He is the Son of God who died in our place. He was raised from the dead and ascended back to heaven. He has promised to return to the earth a second time. He indwells everyone who has received Him. Through Jesus Christ and the Holy Spirit we have a personal relationship with the Father now and forever.

1. Circle key words and phrases in the following Scriptures.

   The Son is the radiance of God's glory and the exact representation of his being, sustaining all things by his powerful word. After he had provided purification for sins, he sat down at the right hand of the Majesty in heaven. HEBREWS 1:3

   In the beginning was the Word, and the Word was with God, and the Word was God. . . . The Word became flesh and made his dwelling among us. JOHN 1:1, 14

   For in Christ all the fullness of the Deity lives in bodily form, and you have been given fullness in Christ, who is the head over every power and authority. COLOSSIANS 2:9–10

   Regarding his Son, who as to his human nature was a descendant of David, and who through the Spirit of holiness was declared with power to be the Son of God by his resurrection from the dead: Jesus Christ our Lord. ROMANS 1:3–4

   For there is one God and one mediator between God and men, the man Christ Jesus, who gave himself as a ransom for all. 1 TIMOTHY 2:5–6

   * *While we wait for the blessed hope—the glorious appearing of our great God and Savior, Jesus Christ, who gave himself for us to redeem us from all wickedness and to purify for himself a people that are his very own, eager to do what is good.* TITUS 2:13–14

2. In the above Scriptures, what do we learn about (answer briefly):

   Who is Jesus Christ?
   What has He done for us?

3. Do a verse study using the form on the next page.

4. Memorize Titus 2:13–14.

28

Verse Study Form

Using the suggested memory verse marked with an asterisk from the opposite page, complete this verse study form.

1. Verse reference _____

2. List two key words and define them.
Key Word _____
Definition _____

_____

Key Word _____
Definition _____

_____

3. What does the verse say?
(Paraphrase—Rewrite the verse in your own words.)

_____

_____

_____

_____

_____

_____

4. How can you apply the truth of this verse to your life today?

_____

_____

_____

_____

_____

Closing (Prayer time and assignment for next week)

nine
The Holy Spirit—His Works

God indwells us by His Holy Spirit. The Holy Spirit wants to control our lives, give us a dynamic for living and make us more like Jesus each day.

1. Circle key words and phrases in the following Scriptures.

Do not get drunk on wine, which leads to debauchery. Instead, be filled with the Spirit.   EPHESIANS 5:18

After they prayed, the place where they were meeting was shaken. And they were all filled with the Holy Spirit and spoke the word of God boldly.
                                                        ACTS 4:31

For God did not give us a spirit of timidity, but a spirit of power, of love and of self-discipline.   2 TIMOTHY 1:7

* *But the fruit of the Spirit is love, joy, peace, patience, kindness, goodness, faithfulness, gentleness and self-control. Against such things there is no law.*
                                                   GALATIANS 5:22–23

And we, who with unveiled faces all reflect the Lord's glory, are being transformed into his likeness with ever-increasing glory, which comes from the Lord, who is the Spirit.   2 CORINTHIANS 3:18

Since we live by the Spirit, let us keep in step with the Spirit. Let us not become conceited, provoking and envying each other.   GALATIANS 5:25–26

2. What do we learn about the Holy Spirit in (answer briefly):

Ephesians 5:18   Galatians 5:22–23
Acts 4:31   2 Corinthians 3:18
2 Timothy 1:7   Galatians 5:25–26

3. Do a verse study using the form on the next page.

4. Memorize Galatians 5:22–23.

Verse Study Form

Using the suggested memory verse marked with an asterisk from the opposite page, complete this verse study form.

1. Verse reference _____

2. List two key words and define them.
Key Word _____
Definition _____
_____

Key Word _____
Definition _____
_____

3. What does the verse say?
(Paraphrase—Rewrite the verse in your own words.)

_____
_____
_____
_____
_____
_____

4. How can you apply the truth of this verse to your life today?

_____
_____
_____
_____
_____
_____

Closing (Prayer time and assignment for next week)

ten Trusting in God

As you study the Scriptures you will discover what it means to place your full trust in God. The following Scriptures speak about the "fear" of the Lord and what will result when we have a trusting respect for His authority.

1. Circle key words and phrases in the following Scriptures.

> *The* LORD *confides in those who fear him; he makes his covenant known to them.* PSALM 25:14

> *But the eyes of the* LORD *are on those who fear him, on those whose hope is in his unfailing love.* PSALM 33:18

> * *The angel of the* LORD *encamps around those who fear him, and he delivers them. . . . Fear the* LORD*, you his saints, for those who fear him lack nothing.* PSALM 34:7, 9

> *He fulfills the desires of those who fear him; he hears their cry and saves them.* PSALM 145:19

> *The fear of the* LORD *is the beginning of knowledge, but fools despise wisdom and discipline. . . . The fear of the* LORD *is the beginning of wisdom, and knowledge of the Holy One is understanding.* PROVERBS 1:7; 9:10

> *Humility and the fear of the* LORD *bring wealth and honor and life.* PROVERBS 22:4

2. What do we learn about trust in (answer briefly):

    Psalm 25:14   *Psalm 145:19*
    Psalm 33:18   *Proverbs 1:7 and 9:10*
    Psalm 34:7, 9   *Proverbs 22:4*

3. Do a verse study using the form on the next page.

4. Memorize Psalm 34:7, 9.

Verse Study Form

Using the suggested memory verse marked with an asterisk from the opposite page, complete this verse study form.

1. Verse reference _____

2. List two key words and define them.
Key Word _____
Definition _____
_____

Key Word _____
Definition _____
_____

3. What does the verse say?
(Paraphrase—Rewrite the verse in your own words.)

_____
_____
_____
_____
_____

4. How can you apply the truth of this verse to your life today?

_____
_____
_____
_____
_____

Closing (Prayer time and assignment for next week)

eleven
Discipleship

A disciple is a "learner—a follower of Christ." A true disciple will recognize Jesus Christ as Lord and be willing to put Him ahead of every pursuit in life.

I. Circle key words and phrases in the following Scriptures.

* *And anyone who does not carry his cross and follow me cannot be my disciple.*
LUKE 14:27

In the same way, any of you who does not give up everything he has cannot be my disciple.
LUKE 14:33

This is to my Father's glory, that you bear much fruit, showing yourselves to be my disciples.
JOHN 15:8

By this all men will know that you are my disciples, if you love one another.
JOHN 13:35

To the Jews who had believed him, Jesus said, "If you hold to my teaching, you are really my disciples."
JOHN 8:31

A student is not above his teacher, nor a servant above his master.
MATTHEW 10:24

2. What do we learn about discipleship in (answer briefly):

Luke 14:27	*John 13:35*
Luke 14:33	*John 8:31*
John 15:8	*Matthew 10:24*

3. Do a verse study using the form on the next page.

4. Memorize Luke 14:27.

Verse Study Form

Using the suggested memory verse marked with an asterisk from the opposite page, complete this verse study form.

1. Verse reference _____

2. List two key words and define them.
Key Word _____
Definition _____
_____

Key Word _____
Definition _____
_____

3. What does the verse say?
(Paraphrase—Rewrite the verse in your own words.)

_____
_____
_____
_____
_____
_____

4. How can you apply the truth of this verse to your life today?

_____
_____
_____
_____
_____
_____

Closing (Prayer time and assignment for next week)

twelve
Obedience

God gave us His Word not only to increase our knowledge about Him but to change our lives. Only as we apply truth to our lives—obey the Scripture—will there be any significant changes made.

I. Circle key words and phrases in the following Scriptures.

Why do you call me, "Lord, Lord," and do not do what I say? LUKE 6:46

Now all has been heard; here is the conclusion of the matter: Fear God and keep his commandments, for this is the whole duty of man.
ECCLESIASTES 12:13

* *Love the LORD your God with all your heart and with all your soul and with all your strength. These commandments that I give you today are to be upon your hearts.* DEUTERONOMY 6:5–6

Whoever has my commands and obeys them, he is the one who loves me. He who loves me will be loved by my Father, and I too will love him and show myself to him. JOHN 14:21

The man who says, "I know him," but does not do what he commands is a liar, and the truth is not in him. 1 JOHN 2:4

This is love for God: to obey his commands. And his commands are not burdensome. 1 JOHN 5:3

2. What do we learn about obedience in (answer briefly):

Luke 6:46	*John 14:21*
Ecclesiastes 12:13	*1 John 2:4*
Deuteronomy 6:5–6	*1 John 5:3*

3. Do a verse study using the form on the next page.

4. Memorize Deuteronomy 6:5–6.

Verse Study Form

Using the suggested memory verse marked with an asterisk from the opposite page, complete this verse study form.

1. Verse reference _____

2. List two key words and define them.
Key Word _____
Definition _____

_____

Key Word _____
Definition _____

_____

3. What does the verse say?
(Paraphrase—Rewrite the verse in your own words.)

_____

_____

_____

_____

_____

_____

4. How can you apply the truth of this verse to your life today?

_____

_____

_____

_____

_____

_____

Closing (Prayer time and assignment for next week)

thirteen
The Church

The Bible clearly states that believers should meet together regularly for prayer, worship, teaching, fellowship and mutual encouragement. God never intended that we walk alone in our faith. Involvement in a local church is vital to our growth in Christ.

1. Circle key words and phrases in the following Scriptures.

> *They devoted themselves to the apostles' teaching and to the fellowship, to the breaking of bread and to prayer.* ACTS 2:42

> * *For where two or three come together in my name, there am I with them.* MATTHEW 18:20

> *Carry each other's burdens, and in this way you will fulfill the law of Christ.* GALATIANS 6:2

> *Let us not give up meeting together, as some are in the habit of doing, but let us encourage one another—and all the more as you see the Day approaching.* HEBREWS 10:25

> *A new command I give you: Love one another. As I have loved you, so you must love one another. By this all men will know that you are my disciples, if you love one another.* JOHN 13:34–35

> *It was he who gave some to be apostles, some to be prophets, some to be evangelists, and some to be pastors and teachers, to prepare God's people for works of service, so that the body of Christ may be built up until we all reach unity in the faith and in the knowledge of the Son of God and become mature, attaining to the whole measure of the fullness of Christ.* EPHESIANS 4:11–13

2. What do we learn about life in fellowship with each other from these verses (answer briefly):

Acts 2:42	Hebrews 10:25
Matthew 18:20	John 13:34–35
Galatians 6:2	Ephesians 4:11–13

3. Do a verse study using the form on the next page.

4. Memorize Matthew 18:20.

Verse Study Form

Using the suggested memory verse marked with an asterisk from the opposite page, complete this verse study form.

1. Verse reference _____

2. List two key words and define them.
Key Word _____
Definition _____

_____

Key Word _____
Definition _____

_____

3. What does the verse say?
(Paraphrase—Rewrite the verse in your own words.)

_____

_____

_____

_____

_____

_____

4. How can you apply the truth of this verse to your life today?

_____

_____

_____

_____

_____

Closing (Prayer time and assignment for next week)

fourteen
Satan the Tempter

From the day that you received Jesus Christ as Savior, you entered into spiritual warfare. Your enemy is the devil, and he will do everything in his power to make you a discouraged, doubting, defeated Christian. Be aware of his tricks and trust in the Lord Jesus Christ for victory.

1. Circle key words and phrases in the following Scriptures.

Jesus, full of the Holy Spirit, returned from the Jordan and was led by the Spirit in the desert, where for forty days he was tempted by the devil. He ate nothing during those days, and at the end of them he was hungry.
LUKE 4:1–2

Simon, Simon, Satan has asked to sift you as wheat. But I have prayed for you, Simon, that your faith may not fail. And when you have turned back, strengthen your brothers.
LUKE 22:31–32

* *Watch and pray so that you will not fall into temptation. The spirit is willing, but the body is weak.*
MATTHEW 26:41

Be self-controlled and alert. Your enemy the devil prowls around like a roaring lion looking for someone to devour.
1 PETER 5:8

Submit yourselves, then, to God. Resist the devil, and he will flee from you.
JAMES 4:7

Put on the full armor of God so that you can take your stand against the devil's schemes.
EPHESIANS 6:11

2. What do we learn about Satan and temptation in (answer briefly):

Luke 4:1–2   1 Peter 5:8
Luke 22:31–32   James 4:7
Matthew 26:41   Ephesians 6:11

3. Do a verse study using the form on the next page.

4. Memorize Matthew 26:41.

Verse Study Form

Using the suggested memory verse marked with an asterisk from the opposite page, complete this verse study form.

1. Verse reference _____

2. List two key words and define them.
Key Word _____
Definition _____
_____

Key Word _____
Definition _____
_____

3. What does the verse say?
(Paraphrase—Rewrite the verse in your own words.)

_____
_____
_____
_____
_____
_____

4. How can you apply the truth of this verse to your life today?

_____
_____
_____
_____
_____
_____

Closing (Prayer time and assignment for next week)

fifteen
Victory

All believers are subject to temptation. But victory can be yours if you use the resources available.

1. Circle key words and phrases in the following Scriptures.

No temptation has seized you except what is common to man. And God is faithful; he will not let you be tempted beyond what you can bear. But when you are tempted, he will also provide a way out so that you can stand up under it. 1 CORINTHIANS 10:13

You, dear children, are from God and have overcome them, because the one who is in you is greater than the one who is in the world. 1 JOHN 4:4

This is love for God: to obey his commands. And his commands are not burdensome, for everyone born of God overcomes the world. This is the victory that has overcome the world, even our faith. 1 JOHN 5:3–4

So I say, live by the Spirit, and you will not gratify the desires of the sinful nature. GALATIANS 5:16

* *I have hidden your word in my heart that I might not sin against you.* PSALM 119:11

But thanks be to God, who always leads us in triumphal procession in Christ and through us spreads everywhere the fragrance of the knowledge of him. 2 CORINTHIANS 2:14

2. What do we learn about victory in (answer briefly):

1 Corinthians 10:13	Galatians 5:16
1 John 4:4	Psalm 119:11
1 John 5:3–4	2 Corinthians 2:14

3. Do a verse study using the form on the next page.

4. Memorize Psalm 119:11.

Verse Study Form

Using the suggested memory verse marked with an asterisk from the opposite page, complete this verse study form.

1. Verse reference _____

2. List two key words and define them.
Key Word _____
Definition _____
_____

Key Word _____
Definition _____
_____

3. What does the verse say?
(Paraphrase—Rewrite the verse in your own words.)

_____
_____
_____
_____
_____
_____

4. How can you apply the truth of this verse to your life today?

_____
_____
_____
_____
_____
_____

Closing (Prayer time and assignment for next week)

sixteen
God's Forgiveness

It is God's desire that every believer live a victorious Christian life. Yet, God knows that there will be times when we will yield to sin and temptation. In His graciousness God has provided a way for us, through confession, to be forgiven and cleansed from all sin.

1. Circle key words and phrases in the following Scriptures.

   My dear children, I write this to you so that you will not sin. But if anybody does sin, we have one who speaks to the Father in our defense—Jesus Christ, the Righteous One. 1 JOHN 2:1

   For we do not have a high priest who is unable to sympathize with our weaknesses, but we have one who has been tempted in every way, just as we are—yet was without sin. Let us then approach the throne of grace with confidence, so that we may receive mercy and find grace to help us in our time of need. HEBREWS 4:15–16

   He who conceals his sins does not prosper, but whoever confesses and renounces them finds mercy. PROVERBS 28:13

   * *If we confess our sins, he is faithful and just and will forgive us our sins and purify us from all unrighteousness.* 1 JOHN 1:9

   Then I acknowledged my sin to you and did not cover up my iniquity. I said, "I will confess my transgressions to the LORD"—and you forgave the guilt of my sin. PSALM 32:5

   As far as the east is from the west, so far has he removed our transgressions from us. PSALM 103:12

2. What do we learn about forgiveness in (answer briefly):

1 John 2:1	1 John 1:9
Hebrews 4:15–16	Psalm 32:5
Proverbs 28:13	Psalm 103:12

3. Do a verse study using the form on the next page.

4. Memorize 1 John 1:9.

44

Verse Study Form

Using the suggested memory verse marked with an asterisk from the opposite page, complete this verse study form.

1. Verse reference _____

2. List two key words and define them.
Key Word _____
Definition _____

_____

Key Word _____
Definition _____

_____

3. What does the verse say?
(Paraphrase—Rewrite the verse in your own words.)

_____

_____

_____

_____

_____

_____

4. How can you apply the truth of this verse to your life today?

_____

_____

_____

_____

_____

_____

Closing (Prayer time and assignment for next week)

seventeen

Praise & Thanksgiving

Praise and thanksgiving please God. On occasion, we ought to take our entire prayer time to tell God how much we appreciate all that He is doing for us each and every day.

1. Circle key words and phrases in the following Scriptures.

He who sacrifices thank offerings honors me, and he prepares the way so that I may show him the salvation of God. PSALM 50:23

I will praise God's name in song and glorify him with thanksgiving. This will please the LORD more than an ox, more than a bull with its horns and hoofs. PSALM 69:30–31

Praise the LORD. Give thanks to the LORD, for he is good; his love endures forever. PSALM 106:1

Let them give thanks to the LORD for his unfailing love and his wonderful deeds for men. PSALM 107:8

Do not be anxious about anything, but in everything, by prayer and petition, with thanksgiving, present your requests to God. PHILIPPIANS 4:6

* *Be joyful always; pray continually; give thanks in all circumstances, for this is God's will for you in Christ Jesus.* 1 THESSALONIANS 5:16–18

2. What do we learn about praise and thanksgiving in (answer briefly):

Psalm 50:23   Psalm 107:8
Psalm 69:30–31   Philippians 4:6
Psalm 106:1   1 Thessalonians 5:16–18

3. Do a verse study using the form on the next page.

4. Memorize 1 Thessalonians 5:16–18.

Verse Study Form

Using the suggested memory verse marked with an asterisk from the opposite page, complete this verse study form.

1. Verse reference _____

2. List two key words and define them.
Key Word _____
Definition _____

_____

Key Word _____
Definition _____

_____

3. What does the verse say?
(Paraphrase—Rewrite the verse in your own words.)

_____

_____

_____

_____

_____

_____

4. How can you apply the truth of this verse to your life today?

_____

_____

_____

_____

_____

Closing (Prayer time and assignment for next week)

eighteen
Guidance

Let God direct your daily path and you will save a lot of heartache, wasted time, dead-end roads and wrong turns in your Christian life. God sees things from a different perspective.

1. Circle key words and phrases in the following Scriptures.

Show me your ways, O LORD, teach me your paths; guide me in your truth and teach me, for you are God my Savior, and my hope is in you all day long.   PSALM 25:4–5

He guides the humble in what is right and teaches them his way.
                                        PSALM 25:9

I will instruct you and teach you in the way you should go; I will counsel you and watch over you.   PSALM 32:8

Let the morning bring me word of your unfailing love, for I have put my trust in you. Show me the way I should go, for to you I lift up my soul.
                                        PSALM 143:8

* *Trust in the LORD with all your heart and lean not on your own under-standing; in all your ways acknowledge him, and he will make your paths straight.*   PROVERBS 3:5–6

The LORD will guide you always; he will satisfy your needs in a sun-scorched land and will strengthen your frame. You will be like a well-watered garden, like a spring whose waters never fail.   ISAIAH 58:11

2. What do we learn about guidance in (answer briefly):

> Psalm 25:4–5   Psalm 143:8
> Psalm 25:9   Proverbs 3:5–6
> Psalm 32:8   Isaiah 58:11

3. Do a verse study using the form on the next page.

4. Memorize Proverbs 3:5–6.

Verse Study Form

Using the suggested memory verse marked with an asterisk from the opposite page, complete this verse study form.

1. Verse reference _____

2. List two key words and define them.
Key Word _____
Definition _____
_____

Key Word _____
Definition _____
_____

3. What does the verse say?
(Paraphrase—Rewrite the verse in your own words.)
_____
_____
_____
_____
_____
_____

4. How can you apply the truth of this verse to your life today?
_____
_____
_____
_____
_____
_____

Closing (Prayer time and assignment for next week)

nineteen
Adversity

In many respects, the Christian life is a life of testing. We can expect trials because God, through adverse situations, takes out of our lives things that are not pleasing to Him. But trials should never be viewed as punishment.

1. Circle key words and phrases in the following Scriptures.

Consider it pure joy, my brothers, whenever you face trials of many kinds, because you know that the testing of your faith develops perseverance. Perseverance must finish its work so that you may be mature and complete, not lacking anything.   JAMES 1:2–4

Not only so, but we also rejoice in our sufferings, because we know that suffering produces perseverance; perseverance, character; and character, hope.   ROMANS 5:3–4

* *And we know that in all things God works for the good of those who love him, who have been called according to his purpose.*   ROMANS 8:28

Naked I came from my mother's womb, and naked I will depart. The LORD gave and the LORD has taken away; may the name of the LORD be praised. . . . But he knows the way that I take; when he has tested me, I will come forth as gold.   JOB 1:21; 23:10

We are hard pressed on every side, but not crushed; perplexed, but not in despair; persecuted, but not abandoned; struck down, but not destroyed.   2 CORINTHIANS 4:8–9

Therefore we do not lose heart. Though outwardly we are wasting away, yet inwardly we are being renewed day by day. For our light and momentary troubles are achieving for us an eternal glory that far out-weighs them all.   2 CORINTHIANS 4:16–17

2. What do we learn about adversity in (answer briefly):

James 1:2–4	Job 1:21 and 23:10
Romans 5:3–4	2 Corinthians 4:8–9
Romans 8:28	2 Corinthians 4:16–17

3. Do a verse study using the form on the next page.

4. Memorize Romans 8:28.

Verse Study Form

Using the suggested memory verse marked with an asterisk from the opposite page, complete this verse study form.

1. Verse reference _____

2. List two key words and define them.
Key Word _____
Definition _____

_____

Key Word _____
Definition _____

_____

3. What does the verse say?
(Paraphrase—Rewrite the verse in your own words.)

_____

_____

_____

_____

_____

_____

4. How can you apply the truth of this verse to your life today?

_____

_____

_____

_____

_____

_____

Closing (Prayer time and assignment for next week)

twenty
Discipline

There are times when God corrects us. Because of His love for us, He will sometimes bring a measure of discipline into our lives.

1. Circle key words and phrases in the following Scriptures.

> *Blessed is the man whom God corrects; so do not despise the discipline of the Almighty.*   JOB 5:17

> *Blessed is the man you discipline, O LORD, the man you teach from your law.*   PSALM 94:12

> *My son, do not despise the LORD's discipline and do not resent his rebuke, because the LORD disciplines those he loves, as a father the son he delights in.*   PROVERBS 3:11–12

> *And you have forgotten that word of encouragement that addresses you as sons: "My son, do not make light of the Lord's discipline, and do not lose heart when he rebukes you, because the Lord disciplines those he loves, and he punishes everyone he accepts as a son."*   HEBREWS 12:5–6

> * *But if we judged ourselves, we would not come under judgment. When we are judged by the Lord, we are being disciplined so that we will not be condemned with the world.*   1 CORINTHIANS 11:31–32

> *Before I was afflicted I went astray, but now I obey your word. . . . I know, O LORD, that your laws are righteous, and in faithfulness you have afflicted me.*   PSALM 119:67, 75

2. What do we learn about discipline in (answer briefly):

Job 5:17	*Hebrews 12:5–6*
Psalm 94:12	*1 Corinthians 11:31–32*
Proverbs 3:11–12	*Psalm 119:67, 75*

3. Do a verse study using the form on the next page.

4. Memorize 1 Corinthians 11:31–32.

Verse Study Form

Using the suggested memory verse marked with an asterisk from the opposite page, complete this verse study form.

1. Verse reference _____

2. List two key words and define them.
Key Word _____
Definition _____
_____

Key Word _____
Definition _____
_____

3. What does the verse say?
(Paraphrase—Rewrite the verse in your own words.)

_____
_____
_____
_____
_____
_____

4. How can you apply the truth of this verse to your life today?

_____
_____
_____
_____
_____
_____

Closing (Prayer time and assignment for next week)

twenty-one

Self-Denial

Christians have two natures. If we are going to grow in Christ, we must learn to say "No" to the flesh, which is the old nature, and "Yes" to Christ, who lives within us.

1. Circle key words and phrases in the following Scriptures.

I have been crucified with Christ and I no longer live, but Christ lives in me. The life I live in the body, I live by faith in the Son of God, who loved me and gave himself for me.   GALATIANS 2:20

Dear friends, I urge you, as aliens and strangers in the world, to abstain from sinful desires, which war against your soul.   1 PETER 2:11

You were taught, with regard to your former way of life, to put off your old self, which is being corrupted by its deceitful desires; . . . and to put on the new self, created to be like God in true righteousness and holiness.
                    EPHESIANS 4:22, 24

Rather, clothe yourselves with the Lord Jesus Christ, and do not think about how to gratify the desires of the sinful nature.   ROMANS 13:14

* *Then he said to them all: "If anyone would come after me, he must deny himself and take up his cross daily and follow me."*   LUKE 9:23

No, I beat my body and make it my slave so that after I have preached to others, I myself will not be disqualified for the prize.
                    1 CORINTHIANS 9:27

2. What do we learn about self-denial in (answer briefly):

Galatians 2:20	Romans 13:14
1 Peter 2:11	Luke 9:23
Ephesians 4:22, 24	1 Corinthians 9:27

3. Do a verse study using the form on the next page.

4. Memorize Luke 9:23.

Verse Study Form

Using the suggested memory verse marked with an asterisk from the opposite page, complete this verse study form.

1. Verse reference _____

2. List two key words and define them.
Key Word _____
Definition _____
_____

Key Word _____
Definition _____
_____

3. What does the verse say?
(Paraphrase—Rewrite the verse in your own words.)

_____
_____
_____
_____
_____
_____

4. How can you apply the truth of this verse to your life today?

_____
_____
_____
_____
_____
_____

Closing (Prayer time and assignment for next week)

twenty-two

Generosity

The Bible says, "God loves a cheerful giver." The following Scriptures give many reasons for giving generously.

1. Circle key words and phrases in the following Scriptures.

> *But who am I, and who are my people, that we should be able to give as generously as this? Everything comes from you, and we have given you only what comes from your hand.*   1 CHRONICLES 29:14

> *Honor the LORD with your wealth, with the firstfruits of all your crops; then your barns will be filled to overflowing, and your vats will brim over with new wine.*   PROVERBS 3:9–10

* *One man gives freely, yet gains even more; another withholds unduly, but comes to poverty. A generous man will prosper; he who refreshes others will himself be refreshed.*   PROVERBS 11:24–25

> *Give, and it will be given to you. A good measure, pressed down, shaken together and running over, will be poured into your lap. For with the measure you use, it will be measured to you.*   LUKE 6:38

> *Remember this: Whoever sows sparingly will also reap sparingly, and whoever sows generously will also reap generously. Each man should give what he has decided in his heart to give, not reluctantly or under compulsion, for God loves a cheerful giver.*   2 CORINTHIANS 9:6–7

> *In everything I did, I showed you that by this kind of hard work we must help the weak, remembering the words the Lord Jesus himself said: "It is more blessed to give than to receive."*   ACTS 20:35

2. What do we learn about generosity in (answer briefly):

      1 Chronicles 29:14   *Luke 6:38*
      Proverbs 3:9–10   *2 Corinthians 9:6–7*
      Proverbs 11:24–25   *Acts 20:35*

3. Do a verse study using the form on the next page.

4. Memorize Proverbs 11:24–25.

Verse Study Form

Using the suggested memory verse marked with an asterisk from the opposite page, complete this verse study form.

1. Verse reference _____

2. List two key words and define them.
Key Word _____
Definition _____
_____

Key Word _____
Definition _____
_____

3. What does the verse say?
(Paraphrase—Rewrite the verse in your own words.)
_____
_____
_____
_____
_____
_____

4. How can you apply the truth of this verse to your life today?
_____
_____
_____
_____
_____
_____

Closing (Prayer time and assignment for next week)

twenty-three
God's Divine Care

In spite of all the trials, testing and suffering we may face, God still watches over us and meets our every need.

1. Circle key words and phrases in the following Scriptures.

When you pass through the waters, I will be with you; and when you pass through the rivers, they will not sweep over you. When you walk through the fire, you will not be burned; the flames will not set you ablaze.
ISAIAH 43:2

So do not fear, for I am with you; do not be dismayed, for I am your God. I will strengthen you and help you; I will uphold you with my righteous right hand.
ISAIAH 41:10

A righteous man may have many troubles, but the LORD delivers him from them all.
PSALM 34:19

Cast your cares on the LORD and he will sustain you; he will never let the righteous fall.
PSALM 55:22

* *Cast all your anxiety on him because he cares for you.*
1 PETER 5:7

Come to me, all you who are weary and burdened, and I will give you rest. Take my yoke upon you and learn from me, for I am gentle and humble in heart, and you will find rest for your souls.
MATTHEW 11:28–29

2. What do we learn about God's care in (answer briefly):

Isaiah 43:2	Psalm 55:22
Isaiah 41:10	1 Peter 5:7
Psalm 34:19	Matthew 11:28–29

3. Do a verse study using the form on the next page.

4. Memorize 1 Peter 5:7.

Verse Study Form

Using the suggested memory verse marked with an asterisk from the opposite page, complete this verse study form.

1. Verse reference _____

2. List two key words and define them.
Key Word _____
Definition _____
_____

Key Word _____
Definition _____
_____

3. What does the verse say?
(Paraphrase—Rewrite the verse in your own words.)

_____
_____
_____
_____
_____
_____

4. How can you apply the truth of this verse to your life today?

_____
_____
_____
_____
_____
_____

Closing (Prayer time and assignment for next week)

twenty-four
Love

All around us are people starving for love. May our love reach out to them and help meet their need.

1. Circle key words and phrases in the following Scriptures.

A new command I give you: Love one another. As I have loved you, so you must love one another. JOHN 13:34

* *Love must be sincere. Hate what is evil; cling to what is good. Be devoted to one another in brotherly love. Honor one another above yourselves.* ROMANS 12:9–10

Be completely humble and gentle; be patient, bearing with one another in love. Make every effort to keep the unity of the Spirit through the bond of peace. EPHESIANS 4:2–3

We know that we have passed from death to life, because we love our brothers. Anyone who does not love remains in death. 1 JOHN 3:14

If anyone has material possessions and sees his brother in need but has no pity on him, how can the love of God be in him? Dear children, let us not love with words or tongue but with actions and in truth. 1 JOHN 3:17–18

And over all these virtues put on love, which binds them all together in perfect unity. COLOSSIANS 3:14

2. What do we learn about love in (answer briefly):

John 13:34   1 John 3:14
Romans 12:9–10   1 John 3:17–18
Ephesians 4:2–3   Colossians 3:14

3. Do a verse study using the form on the next page.

4. Memorize Romans 12:9–10.

Verse Study Form

Using the suggested memory verse marked with an asterisk from the opposite page, complete this verse study form.

1. Verse reference _____

2. List two key words and define them.
Key Word _____
Definition _____
_____

Key Word _____
Definition _____
_____

3. What does the verse say?
(Paraphrase—Rewrite the verse in your own words.)

_____
_____
_____
_____
_____
_____

4. How can you apply the truth of this verse to your life today?

_____
_____
_____
_____
_____

Closing (Prayer time and assignment for next week)

twenty-five
Humility

It is natural for a person to want recognition. We want to achieve much in this life. The following Scriptures give us insights on the proper balance of humility in our lives.

1. Circle key words and phrases in the following Scriptures.

*Pride only breeds quarrels, but wisdom is found in those who take advice.
. . . Pride goes before destruction, a haughty spirit before a fall.*
                                                                    PROVERBS 13:10; 16:18

A man's pride brings him low, but a man of lowly spirit gains honor.
                                                                    PROVERBS 29:23

For everyone who exalts himself will be humbled, and he who humbles him-self will be exalted.   LUKE 14:11

* *But he gives us more grace. That is why Scripture says: "God opposes the proud but gives grace to the humble." . . . Humble yourselves before the Lord, and he will lift you up.*   JAMES 4:6, 10

Humility and the fear of the LORD bring wealth and honor and life.
                                                                    PROVERBS 22:4

"Has not my hand made all these things, and so they came into being?" declares the LORD. "This is the one I esteem: he who is humble and contrite in spirit, and trembles at my word."   ISAIAH 66:2

2. What do we learn about humility in (answer briefly):

Proverbs 13:10 and 16:18	*James 4:6, 10*
Proverbs 29:23	*Proverbs 22:4*
Luke 14:11	*Isaiah 66:2*

3. Do a verse study using the form on the next page.

4. Memorize James 4:6–10.

Verse Study Form

Using the suggested memory verse marked with an asterisk from the opposite page, complete this verse study form.

1. Verse reference _____

2. List two key words and define them.
Key Word _____
Definition _____

_____

Key Word _____
Definition _____

_____

3. What does the verse say?
(Paraphrase—Rewrite the verse in your own words.)

_____

_____

_____

_____

_____

_____

4. How can you apply the truth of this verse to your life today?

_____

_____

_____

_____

_____

_____

Closing (Prayer time and assignment for next week)

twenty-six

Honesty

Honesty is essential in building strong personal relationships. We must be able to trust each other as Christians. Our credibility is especially important in our witness to nonbelievers. Scripture encourages us to back up our witness with honest behavior.

1. Circle key words and phrases in the following Scriptures.

> *Rather, we have renounced secret and shameful ways; we do not use deception, nor do we distort the word of God. On the contrary, by setting forth the truth plainly we commend ourselves to every man's conscience in the sight of God.*   2 CORINTHIANS 4:2

> *Do not lie to each other, since you have taken off your old self with its practices.*   COLOSSIANS 3:9

> *Do not repay anyone evil for evil. Be careful to do what is right in the eyes of everybody.*   ROMANS 12:17

> * *For we are taking pains to do what is right, not only in the eyes of the Lord but also in the eyes of men.*   2 CORINTHIANS 8:21

> *The LORD abhors dishonest scales, but accurate weights are his delight. . . . The integrity of the upright guides them, but the unfaithful are destroyed by their duplicity.*   PROVERBS 11:1, 3

> *An evil man is trapped by his sinful talk, but a righteous man escapes trouble. . . . A truthful witness gives honest testimony, but a false witness tells lies.*   PROVERBS 12:13, 17

2. What do we learn about honesty in (answer briefly):

> 2 Corinthians 4:2   2 Corinthians 8:21
> Colossians 3:9   Proverbs 11:1, 3
> Romans 12:17   Proverbs 12:13, 17

3. Do a verse study using the form on the next page.

4. Memorize 2 Corinthians 8:21.

Verse Study Form

Using the suggested memory verse marked with an asterisk from the opposite page, complete this verse study form.

1. Verse reference _____

2. List two key words and define them.
Key Word _____
Definition _____
_____

Key Word _____
Definition _____
_____

3. What does the verse say?
(Paraphrase—Rewrite the verse in your own words.)
_____
_____
_____
_____
_____
_____

4. How can you apply the truth of this verse to your life today?
_____
_____
_____
_____
_____
_____

Closing (Prayer time and assignment for next week)

twenty-seven
Our Hearts

In Scripture, the words *heart*, *thoughts*, *mind*, or *affections* speak about what is inside us. What we are or do daily will be greatly determined by what is in our heart because what is there will lead to action, good or otherwise.

1. Circle key words and phrases in the following Scriptures.

The heart is deceitful above all things and beyond cure. Who can understand it?   JEREMIAH 17:9

He went on: "What comes out of a man is what makes him 'unclean.' For from within, out of men's hearts, come evil thoughts, sexual immorality, theft, murder, adultery, greed, malice, deceit, lewdness, envy, slander, arrogance and folly."   MARK 7:20–22

Above all else, guard your heart, for it is the wellspring of life.
                                                                                        PROVERBS 4:23

If we had forgotten the name of our God or spread out our hands to a foreign god, would not God have discovered it, since he knows the secrets of the heart?   PSALM 44:20–21

* *Search me, O God, and know my heart; test me and know my anxious thoughts. See if there is any offensive way in me, and lead me in the way everlasting.*   PSALM 139:23–24

Create in me a pure heart, O God, and renew a steadfast spirit within me.
                                                                                        PSALM 51:10

2. What do we learn about the heart in (answer briefly):

Jeremiah 17:9	*Psalm 44:20–21*
Mark 7:20–22	*Psalm 139:23–24*
Proverbs 4:23	*Psalm 51:10*

3. Do a verse study using the form on the next page.

4. Memorize Psalm 139:23–24.

Verse Study Form

Using the suggested memory verse marked with an asterisk from the opposite page, complete this verse study form.

1. Verse reference _____

2. List two key words and define them.
Key Word _____
Definition _____
_____

Key Word _____
Definition _____
_____

3. What does the verse say?
(Paraphrase—Rewrite the verse in your own words.)

_____
_____
_____
_____
_____
_____

4. How can you apply the truth of this verse to your life today?

_____
_____
_____
_____
_____
_____

Closing (Prayer time and assignment for next week)

twenty-eight

Our Tongues

The tongue, though it is a very small member of the body, has enormous power for good or evil. It must be controlled continually.

1. Circle key words and phrases in the following Scriptures.

> *All kinds of animals, birds, reptiles and creatures of the sea are being tamed and have been tamed by man, but no man can tame the tongue. It is a restless evil, full of deadly poison.*   JAMES 3:7–8

> *Reckless words pierce like a sword, but the tongue of the wise brings healing. . . . An anxious heart weighs a man down, but a kind word cheers him up.*   PROVERBS 12:18, 25

> *He who guards his mouth and his tongue keeps himself from calamity.*
>   PROVERBS 21:23

> *Whoever would love life and see good days must keep his tongue from evil and his lips from deceitful speech.*   1 PETER 3:10

> *He who guards his lips guards his life, but he who speaks rashly will come to ruin.*   PROVERBS 13:3

> * *Let your conversation be always full of grace, seasoned with salt, so that you may know how to answer everyone.*   COLOSSIANS 4:6

2. What do we learn about the tongue in (answer briefly):

> James 3:7–8   1 Peter 3:10
> Proverbs 12:18, 25   Proverbs 13:3
> Proverbs 21:23   Colossians 4:6

3. Do a verse study using the form on the next page.

4. Memorize Colossians 4:6.

Verse Study Form

Using the suggested memory verse marked with an asterisk from the opposite page, complete this verse study form.

1. Verse reference _____

2. List two key words and define them.
Key Word _____
Definition _____
_____

Key Word _____
Definition _____
_____

3. What does the verse say?
(Paraphrase—Rewrite the verse in your own words.)

_____
_____
_____
_____
_____
_____

4. How can you apply the truth of this verse to your life today?

_____
_____
_____
_____
_____

Closing (Prayer time and assignment for next week)

twenty-nine
Forgiving Others

If we want to be at peace with God and others, then we must learn to forgive others. An unforgiving attitude can lead to a person's ruin.

1. Circle key words and phrases in the following Scriptures.

Jesus said, "Father, forgive them, for they do not know what they are doing."   LUKE 23:34

Then Peter came to Jesus and asked, "Lord, how many times shall I forgive my brother when he sins against me? Up to seven times?" Jesus answered, "I tell you, not seven times, but seventy-seven times."
MATTHEW 18:21–22

Do not judge, and you will not be judged. Do not condemn, and you will not be condemned. Forgive, and you will be forgiven.   LUKE 6:37

And when you stand praying, if you hold anything against anyone, forgive him, so that your Father in heaven may forgive you your sins.
MARK 11:25

* *Be kind and compassionate to one another, forgiving each other, just as in Christ God forgave you.*   EPHESIANS 4:32

Bear with each other and forgive whatever grievances you may have against one another. Forgive as the Lord forgave you.   COLOSSIANS 3:13

2. What do we learn about forgiving others in (answer briefly):

Luke 23:34	*Mark 11:25*
Matthew 18:21–22	*Ephesians 4:32*
Luke 6:37	*Colossians 3:13*

3. Do a verse study using the form on the next page.

4. Memorize Ephesians 4:32.

Verse Study Form

Using the suggested memory verse marked with an asterisk from the opposite page, complete this verse study form.

1. Verse reference _____

2. List two key words and define them.
Key Word _____
Definition _____
_____

Key Word _____
Definition _____
_____

3. What does the verse say?
(Paraphrase—Rewrite the verse in your own words.)

_____
_____
_____
_____
_____

4. How can you apply the truth of this verse to your life today?

_____
_____
_____
_____
_____

Closing (Prayer time and assignment for next week)

thirty
Proper Perspective

We do not know the day or hour, but one day Jesus Christ is coming back again to take us to be with Him forever. The Scriptures clearly tell us how we should live each day as we await His coming.

1. Circle key words and phrases in the following Scriptures.

* *It teaches us to say "No" to ungodliness and worldly passions, and to live self-controlled, upright and godly lives in this present age, while we wait for the blessed hope—the glorious appearing of our great God and Savior, Jesus Christ.* TITUS 2:12–13

 But our citizenship is in heaven. And we eagerly await a Savior from there, the Lord Jesus Christ. PHILIPPIANS 3:20

 When Christ, who is your life, appears, then you also will appear with him in glory. Put to death, therefore, whatever belongs to your earthly nature: sexual immorality, impurity, lust, evil desires and greed, which is idolatry. COLOSSIANS 3:4–5

 And now, dear children, continue in him, so that when he appears we may be confident and unashamed before him at his coming. 1 JOHN 2:28

 Dear friends, now we are children of God, and what we will be has not yet been made known. But we know that when he appears, we shall be like him, for we shall see him as he is. Everyone who has this hope in him purifies himself, just as he is pure. 1 JOHN 3:2–3

 Do not let your hearts be troubled. Trust in God; trust also in me. In my Father's house are many rooms; if it were not so, I would have told you. I am going there to prepare a place for you. And if I go and prepare a place for you, I will come back and take you to be with me that you also may be where I am. JOHN 14:1–3

2. What do we learn about proper perspective in (answer briefly):

Titus 2:12–13	*1 John 2:28*
Philippians 3:20	*1 John 3:2–3*
Colossians 3:4–5	*John 14:1–3*

3. Do a verse study using the form on the next page.

4. Memorize Titus 2:12–13.

Verse Study Form

Using the suggested memory verse marked with an asterisk from the opposite page, complete this verse study form.

1. Verse reference _____

2. List two key words and define them.
Key Word _____
Definition _____
_____

Key Word _____
Definition _____
_____

3. What does the verse say?
(Paraphrase—Rewrite the verse in your own words.)

_____
_____
_____
_____
_____
_____

4. How can you apply the truth of this verse to your life today?

_____
_____
_____
_____
_____

Closing (Prayer time and assignment for next week)

Tips For Leaders

GENERAL GUIDELINES

1. The purpose of each lesson and verse study is to discover what God's Word says, to understand what it means and to apply it to life.

2. A leader talks less than 20% of the time. Guide by skillfully using questions. Remember, this is not a lecture.

3. Maintain good eye contact by looking around the group and not focusing too much on one person.

4. The discussion of the lesson and verse study will take approximately seventy-five minutes. The leader divides the time between the questions and the verse study, emphasizing the importance of having a clear understanding of the important words. The leader keeps the group moving through the questions and the verse study.

5. A good leader will launch the discussion by using the suggested questions at the bottom of each section. Several additional questions may be used to guide the conversation.

   - "What do others think about this?"
   - "Okay, what else?"
   - If a pause (before someone responds) seems long, ask, "Does everyone understand?" If not, read the Scriptures and ask again.
     Definition: To clarify the meaning for the group—"What do we mean by _____?"
     Illustration: To relate concrete life situations—
       "How does this work out in life?"
       "Has anyone observed this? Tell us about it."
       "For example?"
     Personalization: Applying truth to your own life—
       "How have you experienced this?"
     Concentration: Focus attention on the Word of God as the authority for our discussion and decisions.
       "What other Scriptures help us here?"
       "What Scriptures support this idea?"
       "Turn to _____. How does this Scripture help us with our discussion?"

   NOTE: You need not add any comment after a member speaks. Your silence implies neither approval of their reply nor disagreement with it.

6. Let answers be given by all group members in a spontaneous pattern. Don't call on specific people by name or go around the circle for answers.

7. A Good Question:
- Is never answered by "Yes" or "No."
- Has several replies.
- Is simple—easily understood.
- Is short—to the point.

8. To clarify the meaning of a specific point for the group, ask, "What do we mean by _____?"

9. Stick to the study form and topic. If someone introduces some other subject, just say, "We can explore that some other time. Right now let's look at this study," and repeat a good discussion question.

10. If some people seem to dominate the discussion by talking too much, wait until they have finished and then ask, "What does someone else think about this?"

11. Each section in the study should be summarized before moving on to the next section. "Does this cover the subject?" "What is most meaningful about _____ (section title)?" "What is the most valuable lesson from the section?" Summary statements can be made:
- By the Leader—Jot down notes of what is said. At the conclusion, put the main ideas together in a few sentences of summary.
- By a Group Member—Leader assigns one member to summarize; or a question may be asked to evoke a summary:
  "How would you summarize, in one sentence, what we have learned about _____(section's topic)?"

12. Encourage the group members to make specific applications of the Scripture to their own lives.

13. If someone is repeatedly misunderstanding key elements of the study, counsel that individual outside the group meeting.

GROUP PROBLEMS AND WHAT TO DO ABOUT THEM:

1. Too Talkative:
- Ask: "What does someone else think?"
- Talk to them privately about the problem.
- Ask them to listen and ask questions to "help me out" in the next session.
- Assign them the project of listening to summarize.

2. Wrong Answers Given:
- Guide by letting the group comment or by having some more mature Christians in your group who can contribute a biblical foundation to your discussion.
- Ask: "What Scriptures help us here?" or: "Let's look at _____ (reference) and see how this Scripture speaks to our discussion viewpoint."
- Counsel anyone with a special need privately after the meeting.

3. Non-involved:
- Ask: "Anyone want to add something here?"
- "Just those who haven't spoken before on this question."
- Personal encouragement—take time alone with any reticent person.

4. Sidetracks:
- "Sometime that topic would be an interesting study, but right now the question is _____."
- Face the fact: "I think we're off the track." Repeat the launch question for the section.

ADDITIONAL RESPONSIBILITIES FOR A LEADER MAY INCLUDE:

1. Forming the Group:
- Recruit the members and issue invitations.
- Consult with pastoral leadership for suggestions. If your church has been involved in a special evangelistic event or ministry, a personal invitation should be given early to every inquirer who is referred to your local congregation. New members in your church should be included—your pastor may know of some with special needs.
- Invite personal friends and acquaintances. You may have friends in

business or in the neighborhood who would add a different perspective to the group . . . involve them.

- Find mature Christian friends who know and love the Word of God. They will greatly assist the group's understanding by contributing a biblical basis to the discussion.
- Allow for diversity of background among group members to aid the group's understanding.

2. Arranging practical details for the study. Following are a few suggestions:
- Most successful programs are centered in a home. A home provides a warm and friendly atmosphere.
- Use a room not too small or too large for 6–12 people. Proper lighting, ventilation, and temperature are important.
- Seating should be in a circular pattern, with the circle complete if possible.
- Decide ahead of time who will take care of disturbances such as doorbells, telephones and children.
- Serving refreshments is an option. If deemed appropriate, it should be after the study and clearly made optional for persons on a tight schedule.
- The Discovery Group format is designed for a 75-minute meeting. It is suggested that the study not run longer than this even though some individuals may want to spend additional time together.
- *Thirty Discipleship Exercises* has been prepared to form the basis of discussion. The material is a guide—giving the format and discussion questions needed.

3. Manage Time Allotments
Thirty Discipleship Exercises material has a suggested format including time allotments for each lesson. A good leader will attempt to give complete coverage to the material by setting the pace, moving the discussion along and avoiding sidetrack issues.

4. Leader's Preparation
- Do the study and complete the written answers.
- Make notes of additional questions that will be helpful to stimulate conversation.
- Pray regularly for each member of the group.

NOTES

NOTES

NOTES

NOTES

NOTES

NOTES